Boobela,
Worm
and
Potion
Power

Boobela, Worm and Potion Power

Joe Friedman

Illustrated by Sam Childs

Orion
Children's Books

First published in Great Britain in 2008
by Orion Children's Books
This edition first published in Great Britain in 2010
by Orion Children's Books
a division of the Orion Publishing Group Ltd
Orion House
5 Upper St Martin's Lane
London WC2H 9EA
An Hachette UK Company

1 3 5 7 9 10 8 6 4 2

Text copyright © Joe Friedman 2008, 2010
Illustrations copyright © Sam Childs 2008

The rights of Joe Friedman and Sam Childs to be identified as the author
and illustrator of this work respectively have been asserted.

A catalogue record for this book is available from
the British Library.

ISBN 978 1 4440 0045 0

Printed in China

The Orion Publishing Group's policy is to use papers that are natural,
renewable and recyclable products made from wood grown in sustainable forests.
The logging and manufacturing processes are expected to conform to the
environmental regulations of the country of origin.

www.orionbooks.co.uk
www.boobela.com

For my Mum and Dad.
J.F.

For Inga Moore, a dear friend
and sublime illustrator.
S.C.

Gran's Island

Boobela's World

Boobela's Island

Mountain City

Smoky Mountain

The Great River

Titanic Falls

The Old Woods

Smelly Swamp

Balloon Launch Field

Fjords

Herne Beach

Pipeline Surfing Beach

Scarlet Lake

Boobela's City

Lake

Forbidden Caves

Haunted Castle

Belching Giant

Barton Beach

Contents

The Argument

Boobela was fed up. With everything . . .

Porridge for breakfast.

Tidying up her house and garden.

Having to take baths.

She knew her hair looked like rats
were sleeping in it. And her feet
probably stank. But she didn't care.

11

She glanced at the calendar. There was something written on the date but she couldn't be bothered to read it. It was just too hot. It had been for days.

She was supposed to meet Worm in the garden at ten for dowsing practice. This was part of Worm's new timetable for her. It was now half past. She knew Worm would go on about how she'd missed her practice and what a mess the garden was. She threw on a dirty T-shirt and went out.

Worm was sheltering under a leafy plant. He looked hot and irritated.

"What time do you call this?" he asked. "And what about our new schedule?"

"*Your* new schedule," said Boobela, crossly.

Worm looked at Boobela. "Who got out of bed on the wrong side today?"

Boobela didn't say anything. She didn't want to be jollied out of her mood.

"OK," said Worm. "Be like that. Time to tidy the garden."

"I'm tired of tidying the garden," Boobela shouted. "I don't want to cut the lawn, prune the hedge or pick up the sweet wrappers. In fact, I'd like to cover it all with concrete!"

Worm looked at Boobela coolly. "Go ahead," he said. "But you can say goodbye to our friendship if you do."

Boobela couldn't stop herself. "Who needs your stupid friendship?"

"And who needs a spoilt giant baby?" Worm replied in a temper. With that, he disappeared into the ground.

Boobela was a bit shocked. But also pleased. She'd got rid of that horrible, interfering worm who was always telling her what to do. She kicked a couple of sweet wrappers around the garden and stomped on some grass.

Then she went into the house and put two pizzas in the oven. She threw the boxes onto the floor. When the pizzas were ready, she ate them with her fingers and left the sauce smeared all over her face. She could do whatever she wanted.

I'll go to the Balloon Club, she thought.

It felt strange going down the road without Worm chattering away on her shoulder. But Boobela shrugged it off and walked faster.

* * *

Worm chomped through a mouldy red pepper. He'd come to the compost bin because he thought he could eat and have a gossip.

But all his friends could talk about was how hot it was. Worm was bored. His thoughts wandered to the compost bin in the neighbouring garden. Maybe he could pop over to visit Hannah. Yes. That would be fun. He set off.

* * *

Boobela arrived at the launch field and
was greeted warmly by Kate and Nurgul.

"We're building a balloon pad," said
Kate. "It will hold the basket down
when we're filling the envelope."

"How can I help?" asked Boobela.

"You see that wagon? Could you bring some wood over?" Kate replied.

"Where's Worm?" asked Nurgul.

Boobela hesitated. "He . . . didn't feel like coming today."

"Isn't he well?"

"He's fine," said Boobela curtly. She rushed off to get the wood.

* * *

Worm hadn't seen Hannah since she helped him win his bet with Boobela. He burrowed up into the heap. The first worm he met was her granpa.

"Looking for the young troublemaker, I suppose," he said affectionately.

"You mean Hannah?" asked Worm.

"The very one," said her granpa. "Arthur's the name. Aren't you the worm who won the bet with the giant?"

Worm nodded. "I'm Vivian," he said. "Do you know where Hannah is?"

"A couple of other worms were looking for her earlier. I sent them up to the cabbage patch."

Worm sensed Arthur was making mischief. "But she isn't up by the cabbage patch, is she?"

Arthur threw his head back and laughed. "Clever boy! I get annoyed with everyone asking me where Hannah is. So sometimes I play a little trick on them. You're too smart for me. She's down by the holly bush."

* * *

Worm sat under the holly bush with Hannah. It was shady and cool and the prickly holly leaves kept the birds away.

Worm told Hannah about his adventures since he'd last seen her.

"I wish I had a big friend like Boobela," said Hannah.

"I'm not sure Boobela *is* still my friend," said Worm sadly.

"What happened?" asked Hannah.

Worm told her about their argument.

"She was out of order!" said
Hannah, angrily. "Concrete the garden!
She sounds like a selfish child."

"She is a child," admitted Worm.
"And sometimes she's selfish . . . But
mostly she's really kind and thoughtful.
You have to remember she's only eight
and she's more than twice the size of any
of her friends. *And* she hasn't seen her
parents for months!"

"Really?" said Hannah. She couldn't imagine what it would be like not to see her parents or her granpa every day. It made her feel for Boobela. "That must be terribly hard."

Suddenly, Worm had a thought. "Today's her mother's birthday! That's why she's so irritable . . . She's missing her!"

"You shouldn't leave her alone on a day like this," said Hannah.

"You're right," said Worm.

"Time for a drink," said Kate, back at the launch field.

She got out a large container of lemonade and poured out four glasses. Boobela was pleased to be with her friends but something was missing. Not some*thing*. Some*one*.

"I had a fight with Worm this morning," she confessed. "I was fed up and I said lots of horrible things. Now I'm worried I'll never see him again."

"Was this your first argument?" asked Sophie.

Boobela nodded, her heart heavy.

"The first is always the worst," said Nurgul. "I have lots of tiffs with my best friend. We always get back together."

"I said I wanted to concrete over the garden. He'll never forgive me."

"Don't you think he'll be missing you too?" asked Kate.

Boobela brightened. "You think he might? Even after what I said?"

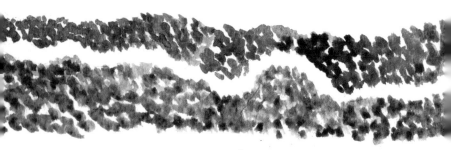

Her friends nodded.

"Maybe I ought to go and find him then . . . and apologize."

"That sounds like a good idea," said Sophie.

Boobela wished she could be home *right now* so she could apologize to Worm and be friends again. The fastest way home was through the centre of town. She remembered how she'd jumped over wagons and cars there. That would be fun as well as fast!

* * *

As Worm tunnelled, he suddenly felt the soil shake.

What was that?

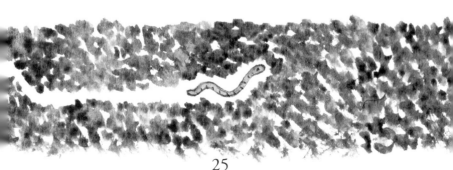

25

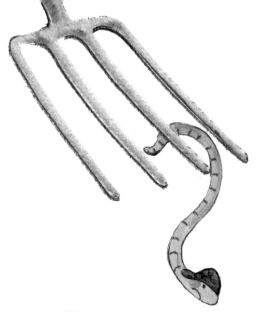

The ground shook again. It was closer this time. Worm couldn't see anything. He was surrounded by soil. What's going on? he worried.

It happened again. Even closer. This time the soil around Worm began to tremble. Worm was frightened.

Suddenly, the soil all around him shifted as a garden fork cut through it. The large prongs almost cut Worm in half. Worm caught his breath. Dive! Dive! he thought. He dived.

* * *

Boobela ran along the road with giant-sized steps. People turned to watch and wave. This was fun. But now the road was clogged with traffic. Boobela heard the sound of a fire engine. A fire!

She tiptoed around two large wagons and then jumped over three carriages. Now she could see it! A factory was burning. Huge flames shot up from the roof. The building was surrounded by steam-powered fire engines. Suddenly, rockets shot out of the building into the air.

She heard a gasp. "It's the fireworks factory!"

Someone cried out from a first floor window. A fireman was trapped in the building! Without thinking, Boobela jumped over the police barrier and ran. She stretched her hands upwards. They were just long enough. The fireman jumped and Boobela caught him.

"Thanks," he said, as more rockets went off.

"No problem," said Boobela as she put him down. She hurried off to get back to Worm.

* * *

Worm caught his breath. He realized he'd been tunnelling through someone's vegetable garden. Just as they were digging it up.

"That was a lucky escape!" he laughed. "What would have happened to Boobela if I'd been cut in half? Come to think of it, what would have happened to me?" He turned to tunnel again towards their garden, glad to be alive.

* * *

Finally, the road ahead was clear.
Boobela was so full of thoughts about
what she wanted to say to Worm that
she didn't look where she was going.

"Ouch!"

she yelped as she tripped over a large stone.

Boobela sprawled on
the ground. Her knee was
bleeding. But what was worse was
her foot. She touched it gently. It
hurt!

She stood up. When her foot
hit the ground, the pain made her
cry out. *How am I going to get home
to Worm?* she thought desperately.

Worm dug as fast as he could. He was
worried it was already dark and Boobela
would give up on him. He was
tunnelling so fast he didn't notice the
nest of tree roots ahead of him.

"Ouch," he cried as he ran into it.
His head was very sore. He looked
around. There were tree roots
everywhere.

The apple tree, Worm thought.
I should have remembered it was in
my path.

Worm started back along the way
he'd just come.

Boobela hopped along the road. People pointed at her and laughed. She didn't care. She had to get back to her friend. But at this speed, it would take for ever.

A big fire-engine stopped in front of her.

"Hey, little lady," shouted the fireman she had saved earlier. "Need a lift?"

* * *

Worm's head ached. The apple tree roots were everywhere. It had taken for ever to get around them.

I've got to go on, he thought. Boobela needs me. He started tunnelling upwards.

* * *

Boobela waved at the fireman as he drove off. It had been fun lying on top of the ladders. She hopped into the garden. It was almost dark. She was very worried Worm wouldn't be there.

"Worm!" she called. "Worm!"

There was no response. Boobela felt awful. Maybe Worm would never come back!

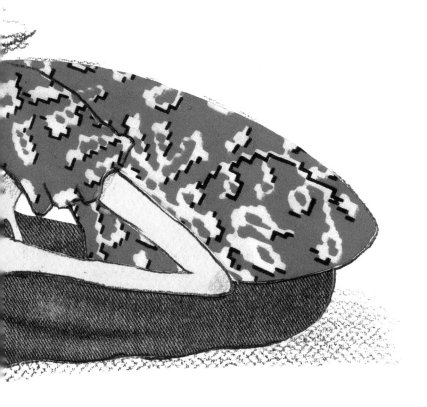

She bent over and pulled up some
weeds, then picked up some sweet
wrappers. "Worm!" she called more
urgently.

* * *

Worm stuck his head out of the ground.
Boobela was sitting there with her head
in her hands. Her shorts were torn and
her foot looked swollen.

"What happened to you?" he asked.

Boobela sighed with relief. She bent over to get near Worm.

"I'm really sorry for the way I spoke to you this morning," she said. "I would never concrete the garden."

"I know that," said Worm. "I should have been more understanding. It's hard to have to be so grown-up when you're only eight. And I know why you're so upset."

"You do?" said Boobela, astonished.

"Today's your mother's birthday!"

Boobela suddenly looked very sad. "Is it the twelfth?" she asked. Then she thought for a moment. "You're right! I wish I could give her a big hug."

"Why don't you close your eyes and imagine it," suggested Worm.

Boobela did. A big smile came over her face.

"That was nice," she said.

Boobela put a sweet wrapper in her pocket and shook Worm's tail.

"Friends?" she asked.

"Always," said Worm. "At least until our next argument . . ."

"Let's not make it too soon," Boobela replied. She pointed at her foot and knee. "I don't think I could survive another one."

Worm thought about his sore head and the garden fork. "I'm not sure I would either," he laughed.

Scarlet Lake

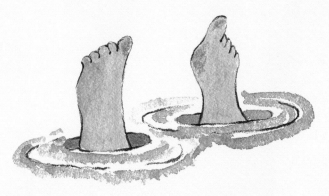

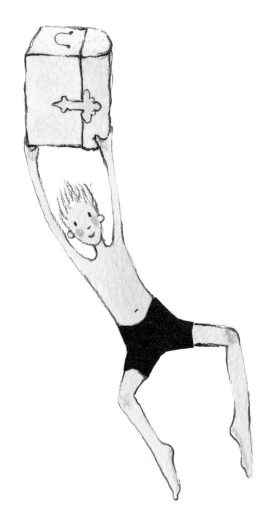

The advertisement jumped out at
Boobela. It could have been written for
her. She'd never been able to have
swimming lessons with other children
because she was too big for baby pools.
Then, when she was older, she'd felt shy
about wearing a swim suit because she
was a giant and ashamed she couldn't
swim. This was her chance to catch up!

But what about Worm? He hated water.

"Don't worry about me," said Worm, who had been reading over Boobela's shoulder. "I've heard the soil at Scarlet Lake tastes delicious . . ."

"Great!" shouted Boobela, jumping up.

* * *

Boobela stood at the edge of the lake. It was surrounded by bushes with red flowers. They were reflected in the water, colouring it scarlet.

"You're not really going to swim in *that*?" Worm exclaimed. "It's like bathing in blood!"

"More like a lovely red bubble bath!" laughed Boobela.

She bent down and stuck her hand in the water. She shivered. "A very cold bubble bath!"

Boobela heard someone behind her. A boy had arrived. He was followed by a tall, skinny girl.

"You *must* be older than ten!" the boy said, looking up at Boobela.

"I'm nine next month." She smiled. "I'm big for my age. My name is Boobela. This is my pal Worm. He's not going swimming."

"I'm Sandy," said the boy. "I'm not sure I'm going swimming either. I've had lots of lessons but I can't even doggy paddle. Whenever I get in too deep, I panic."

"I'm allergic to chlorine," said the girl. "I can't swim in pools and there are no lakes near me. My name is Celine."

Then Boobela noticed a small boy standing apart from the three of them. Boobela could see he was very shy. "What's your name?" she asked.

"Omer," he whispered. "I wish I had a worm on my shoulder."

Boobela looked at Worm. He nodded.

"Here," said Boobela, unfastening Worm's matchbox from her shoulder.

Omer was stunned.

"You can have him until we go in the water."

Boobela attached Worm's box to Omer's shoulder. The strap was far too big so she had to adjust it. Omer smiled a toothy grin.

Boobela realized that the only thing the four children had in common was that they couldn't swim. She wondered what it would be like spending a week together.

A tall man with a neatly trimmed beard joined them. "I'm Colin," he said. "I want you to forget everything you know about swimming."

"That will be easy," said Boobela.

The other children giggled.

Making the children laugh made them feel like more of a gang!

Colin led the children over to a tank of water – it was like a low fish tank without any fish.

"We want each of you to choose a buddy. You'll never be alone in the water because your buddy will always be with you."

Sandy chose Celine. Boobela picked Omer.

"We're a funny pair," said Omer looking up at her.

"Yes," said Boobela. "You're a bit big for me!"

Colin put his face in the water and blew a loud raspberry. "Do you think you can do that?" he asked.

Celine and Sandy were not keen.

"I don't like it when my face gets wet," said Omer, quietly.

"What about this?" said Colin. He put just the tip of his mouth in the water and hummed. Bubbles came out of the water.

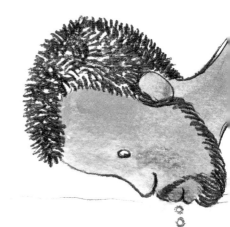

Celine and Sandy gave little nods.
Omer still looked frightened.

"Would it be better if Boobela
put her hand on your back?"

Omer nodded firmly.
"I wouldn't feel so scared."

Sandy stuck his face
in the water.
He blew a
stream of
bubbles out
of his mouth.

Celine tried next. She found it hard to keep her head in the water but eventually she managed long enough to blow some bubbles.

Boobela didn't want Omer to be last. "Your turn," she said.

She put her hand lightly on his back. She could *feel* how frightened he was. All his muscles were wound tight as twisted rope.

Omer leaned towards the water.

"That's close enough!" a very frightened Worm shouted.

Omer stopped what he was doing. He looked at Worm, who had turned very pale.

"I wouldn't have let the water touch you!" he exclaimed.

Worm felt foolish. "I know that," he replied. "It's just that . . . I don't like water."

Omer nodded. He felt the same. "Should I give you to Boobela?"

"Just put me down. I'll check out the local nosh."

Omer carefully put Worm's case down on the ground. Worm crawled onto the soil.

"Good chomping!" said Omer, seriously.

Worm giggled.

Teasing Worm was fun. And Worm was more scared of water than he was!

Feeling much braver, Omer stood up, took a deep breath and stuck his head into the tank, blowing a loud stream of bubbles.

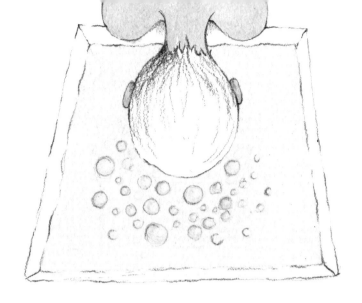

Sandy, Celine and Boobela all applauded and whooped.

Omer was very pleased. "I've never done that before!"

They spent the next hour blowing bubbles.

Fast bubbles, slow bubbles, bubbles while humming, and then nose humming bubbles.

Those were the hardest but Colin taught them a complicated song. The children were thinking so much about remembering the song and humming it, they didn't notice they'd spent the whole morning with their heads in the water learning to breathe out!

* * *

Worm joined them for lunch. Boobela remembered she'd brought Worm's beret to protect him from the sun. She got it out of her rucksack and installed it on Worm's head.

"How's the local nosh?" asked Omer.

Worm smiled. He put on a French accent to match his beret. "Eet 'as beeg, reech cherry flavours wiz a 'int of raspberry."

Everyone laughed. Worm sounded like a dad describing a fine wine.

"No swimming this afternoon," said Colin. "We're going to look for buried treasure. In the lake."

There were six treasure chests for each child. Sandy's were red, Celine's blue, Omer's green and Boobela's yellow. The chests were full of sweets and toys.

Boobela held Omer's hand as they walked out to the first chest. It was only up to Omer's ankles but he inched forward so slowly it took almost ten minutes to get there.

The second chest was up to Omer's knees. Boobela could feel how hard Omer was trying to overcome his fear. Every time a tiny wave lapped against his leg he stopped still and wouldn't move for ages.

The third chest was up to Omer's stomach. When the water got to his hips, he refused to go any further. Boobela was amazed he'd come that far.

"Come on Omer," urged Sandy. "My third chest has a big toy in it! Let's see what's in yours!"

Boobela noticed Omer was holding his breath. She tried to get him to count his breaths so he would relax. He shook his head.

Celine came over and gave Omer a hug. Colin encouraged him. But nothing they said or did made Omer budge. He was just too scared.

Boobela didn't know what to do. She didn't want to go on without her buddy. But she really wanted to find all her treasure and to eat all her sweets!

Then she heard a small voice. Worm! Maybe he'd know what to do! She gave Celine Omer's hand and ran to the shore.

"I've been watching. And thinking," said Worm. "What helped Omer put his head in the water?"

Boobela remembered how when Worm turned pale, Omer's feelings changed.

"When you were more scared than he was!" she whispered.

Worm nodded. "Be scared. Be very scared."

Clever old Worm! "You deserve a very special treat," Boobela said. She put Worm down under a bush and walked very slowly out into the water. When she got to Omer she shivered.

"What's wrong?" asked Omer.

"Worm told me there were monsters in the lake!"

Colin started to correct Boobela, but Boobela looked at him sternly and shook her head. Colin shut up.

"Really?" whispered Omer.

Boobela shivered again. "I'm not going any deeper. I'm scared of monsters!"

Omer looked at Boobela closely. She was more scared than him! Suddenly, he felt more concerned than frightened.

"It's all right," he said, reassuringly. "There aren't any monsters."

"I'm *not* going any deeper."

Omer began to feel braver. "Look," he said. "If I get my next chest, will you promise to get yours?"

Boobela nodded very slowly, as if going deeper in the water was the very last thing she wanted to do. She could see Celine and Sandy hiding their smiles.

Omer took a couple of steps, bent down into the water and got the next chest.

"I need a cuddle," wailed Boobela. She knelt in the water and Omer threw his arms around her. After a bit, she walked out to get her next chest.

Then Boobela pretended to be even more scared.

"NO! NO! MONSTERS!"

she shouted, throwing her arms around.

This made Omer feel even braver. Before long, he had dived in over his head to get the last chest.

"See?" he said. "It's completely safe!"

Celine and Sandy were smiling broadly now.

Boobela knew her trick was making all four of them feel like a gang. She was pleased. But even though pretending to be frightened was fun, she really *was* scared. Because she was so tall, she had to go much further in the lake to get in over her head and find her last chest.

She pointed. "What if the monsters are hiding and waiting for me in the deep water?"

"How many times do I have to tell you," said Omer. "There are no monsters here!"

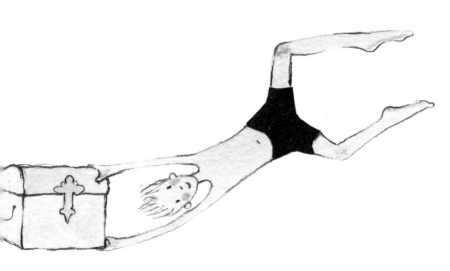

Boobela still felt scared of the deep water. But she didn't want to let the others down.

"OK," she said. "But you all have to promise to stay until I get back from my dive."

The children nodded. Boobela pictured Gran, breathed out very slowly, and let the air rush back into her lungs. Then she plunged into the water.

When she came out everyone cheered. They'd all done it! They'd all gone in over their heads!

* * *

At teatime, Boobela told Celine, Sandy and Omer how clever Worm was. She asked them to look for the blackest, reddest or leafiest loams they could find.

The afternoon was spent playing in the water. Sandy, Celine and Omer loved making a train and diving between Boobela's legs.

In the evening they all sat around a campfire and talked about their treasures and their first day at Scarlet Lake.

"Where's my special treat?" Worm asked Boobela.

"Treat!" exclaimed Boobela. "You deserve more than one."

The children presented the soils they'd found to Worm.

He made a big show of tasting and judging them. Of course, he wore his beret.

About the winner, Worm said, "Ooooh, la, la. Zis ees a very good soil. Eet tastes like ze burnt apricot and smell like ze lovely mouldy tobacco . . ."

* * *

The week seemed to pass in a flash. Colin kept introducing new games so that they never seemed to be learning swimming. Instead they were . . .

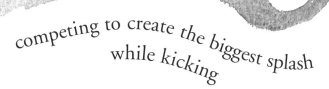

competing to create the biggest splash
while kicking

laying their heads in the water like
a pillow while floating on their backs

or trying not to disturb the water
while moving their arms in the crawl.

Whenever anyone did something special, the children would shout, "Ooooh, la, la!" Then they would fall about laughing.

If Omer was a bit frightened, Sandy or Celine would yell "*Monster!*" and Boobela would pretend to run for the shore. Omer would tell the person off for being mean to his buddy and everyone would crease up. Even Omer was in on the joke.

As she walked home, Boobela thought of all that had happened. She'd had a great time. And now she could swim!

Worm thought about all the great meals he'd had. It was a shame he'd had to leave all those prize-winning soils behind.

Thinking about this made Worm feel hungry.

"Can you put me down?" he asked Boobela. "I need to find something to eat."

Boobela put Worm on the ground. He started to burrow into it.

"Not so fast," Boobela urged. She removed her rucksack and took out seven neatly-labelled bags of soil.

Worm's smile stretched across his whole face. "I thought we'd left them behind!" Then he thought how heavy all that soil would be and how far Boobela had to carry it. "You shouldn't have . . ."

"For my best mate," exclaimed Boobela, "nothing is too good!"

Potion Power

"You got my message," Gran said, pleased.

Boobela knelt so they could give each other a big hug. She'd woken that morning with a dream fresh in her mind. In it, Gran was holding a big invitation. Worm decided that it meant that Gran wanted Boobela to come and visit.

"Is there something wrong?" Boobela asked Gran.

Gran shook her head. "Everything's fine. But before I say why I invited you, let's see if someone else got the call."

Boobela was confused. "Someone else?"

"You're not the only person who's learning magic," said Gran gently.

Boobela face fell. Her shoulders slumped. She'd thought she was Gran's only student! That she was special!

"Of course you're special," Gran said firmly, as if she knew what Boobela was thinking. "But there are very few healers left and I must teach my skills to as many people as I can."

Boobela saw a red-haired girl running towards them. Her clothes matched perfectly and her hair was combed and neat. The girl went straight to Gran and kissed her on the cheek. Then she looked up at Boobela.

"Boobela, I'd like you to meet Sarah," Gran said. "Sarah, Boobela."

Boobela didn't like the idea of anyone else kissing – or learning from – Gran. She felt like kicking Sarah. But she knew Gran would hate that. So reluctantly, she held out her hand.

"I've heard a lot about you," said Sarah. "I think you must be Shirley's best student."

Boobela flinched when Sarah called Gran "Shirley" but then she began to feel a bit better about her.

"Apart from me," Sarah finished.

Boobela's face turned as red as a strawberry ice lolly. She really didn't like this girl!

"Children, children," said Gran. "We've got work to do. Let's get started."

* * *

Boobela gazed over the field of brightly-coloured flowers. "They're beautiful," she gasped.

"Marigolds heal cuts, wounds and infections," said Sarah. "They're good for bee stings and all kinds of skin problems."

"Well done," said Gran. "But I'm sure Boobela knew that too."

Boobela nodded. Though she didn't know anything about marigolds, really.

"What should we do?" asked Boobela.

"Tomorrow is the full moon. It's the best day for making healing potions. At sunrise we'll come here to pick flowers.

We'll only have an hour so we'll have to work fast. Right now, you need to practise."

"I already know how to pick flowers, Gran!" said Boobela.

"This is different," said Gran. "We have to make sure they *want* to be picked. Then our potions will be powerful and strong."

"How do you know whether they want to be picked?" wondered Worm, from Boobela's shoulder.

"You ask them . . ." said Gran.

Worm started to laugh. He stopped suddenly when he realized Gran was serious.

"You mean I have to talk to the flowers?" asked Boobela.

"You don't have to ask out loud," said Gran. "Just in your mind."

"Is it like dowsing?" wondered Worm.

"Of course," said Sarah in a superior voice. "Something inside you tells you what you need to know."

Worm looked at Boobela. He was beginning to dislike this girl too.

Boobela thought about her friend Sophie. She was always getting herself cut or bruised. Now she'd be able to help!

She crouched, looked at a marigold, closed her eyes and asked in her head, *Will you let me pick you? For a healing potion?*

At first, she felt silly trying to talk to a flower. But then she felt a warm glow inside her, and she realized her question had been answered.

"This one says 'yes'," she said to Gran.

Gran put her hand over the flower and closed her eyes. Then she nodded.

"Both of you do twenty more," she said. "Then come back to the house. We'll make dinner and get you to bed early. We'll be up at sunrise."

* * *

Back at the barn, they prepared dinner. Sarah was faster at cutting vegetables, better at arranging them, and when she'd finished, the kitchen looked shiny and her clothes were as clean as when she'd started.

Sarah seemed to be so good at everything. And knew so much! Boobela felt stupid and useless.

"Why does Gran bother with me?" she whispered to Worm.

"Sarah's a know-it-all," Worm whispered back.

This didn't cheer Boobela up. She felt Sarah *did* know it all!

At dinner Boobela felt so gloomy she couldn't say a word. Sarah chattered on about how she was going to be a great healer.

Worm could see that Boobela was forgetting all the things she'd learned and everything she *could* do. After Sarah went home he tried to talk to her. But nothing he said made any difference.

Maybe Gran will do something to help, Worm thought.

But all Gran did was give Boobela a kiss and tell her that she loved her. Worm was very annoyed with Gran. Why hadn't she said more? Couldn't she see how upset Boobela was?

*　*　*

It was still dark when Sarah arrived the next morning. She was wearing different clothes, but everything matched perfectly just as the day before. Boobela looked down at her pick and mix clothes, and sighed.

Gran led them to the field of marigolds. There was a chill in the air. As they arrived, the first rays of the sun touched the flowers. The sight took Boobela's breath away.

"You can feel the magic," Boobela said.

Gran nodded. The she handed Boobela and Sarah a small wicker basket each.

"We only need a cup full. When a flower agrees to be picked, thank it for helping you. And when you pick it, do it quickly."

The three of them worked together. Boobela silently spoke to each flower in turn. Some gave her a bad feeling inside. She left them alone and apologized for disturbing them. Others filled her with happiness.

These would make a powerful potion. She knew flowers didn't live long so she felt very grateful.

As they worked, Boobela became more and more puzzled. Sarah never once noticed how beautiful the flowers were.

* * *

Back at the barn, Gran took the two girls to a room filled with glass jars, creams and potions. She chose six clear bottles and poured a small amount of oil into each one. She gave three to each girl.

Boobela put the marigold flowers into the first bottle, lavender into the second, and St. John's Wort into the third.

Gran put all the bottles in a holder on the window ledge.

The sun streamed through the window into the bottles.

84

"Now what?" asked Boobela.

"We wait until the next full moon," said Gran.

"Why does it have to be so long?" asked Worm.

"The full moon is the best time for starting – and finishing – magical potions."

* * *

A month later, Boobela's balloon lifted into the sky. She was looking forward to seeing Gran again. But not Sarah.

"I can't work her out," said Boobela. "She knows so much and is good at everything, but she doesn't seem to *enjoy* anything."

"I've been thinking about it too," said Worm. "You're both different. You have a huge heart. You know things through your feelings. She's got a big brain and knows everything in her head."

Boobela liked the way Worm had put it. She thought about this during the rest of the flight. She realized that both the head and the heart were important. She needed to use her head more, and Sarah her heart. Maybe Gran had brought them together so they could help each other!

* * *

Gran led Boobela
and Sarah into her
potion room.
Boobela looked
at the bottles on
the window ledge.

The bottles with
marigolds were a
lovely golden
colour, the ones
with St. John's Wort rich
red, and the bottles with lavender were
a deep blue.

"They're beautiful," Boobela
exclaimed.

Gran smiled. "The sun has done its
job, now we need to do ours. Let's start
with the lavender."

Boobela looked at Sarah. She hadn't
noticed the lovely colours of the oils.

What can I do to help her? she thought.

Gran looked at Boobela with surprise. It was almost as if she'd read her mind!

"Now," said Gran. "We filter the lavender flowers from the oil."

Boobela and Sarah used a strainer to do this. Boobela was more awkward than Sarah, but now she didn't mind. These strainers were for normal-sized people!

As they worked, Sarah said, "Lavender helps people to relax and sleep. It's also good when you don't feel like eating."

"How did you get to know so much?" Boobela said.

"I read all about these flowers so I would understand our potions," Sarah replied.

Boobela had read about the marigold, lavender and St. John's Wort in Mum's science books, but she decided not to mention this.

They heated the oil slowly after they'd removed the flowers.

Boobela felt nervous. She understood that Sarah always needed to be the "best" at everything. But she wanted Sarah to try something she wouldn't normally do. Boobela bent down and took a long sniff of the oil.

"It smells really lovely now. Why don't you try?" Boobela urged.

Sarah hesitated. She looked at Boobela's friendly face. Then suddenly she decided and put her nose near the oil.

She took a deep breath. Her face lit up.

"You're right! It's . . . like my gran's perfume. It's *smells* relaxing."

Boobela felt very pleased with herself. Gran winked at her.

They stirred beeswax into the hot oil next. Then they poured the mixture directly into their containers.

"It will harden as it cools," said Gran, "and then it will be ready for you to take away."

* * *

91

The afternoon passed swiftly. Sarah told Boobela all sorts of facts about their potions and Boobela encouraged Sarah to look at and smell things.

"I have to go," said Sarah, sadly. She looked at Boobela. "I've had a great time. Your gran was right. You *are* special!"

Sarah hugged Boobela and Gran and ran off, carrying a bag with her new potions.

"I'll have to go too," said Boobela. "It'll take a while to inflate my balloon."

Gran walked Boobela to her balloon and helped lay it out.

"I was really proud of you today," Gran said. "I know Sarah can be annoying at times . . . And the first night you met her you seemed very down."

"I was," said Boobela. "I couldn't figure her out . . . But Worm put what I was trying to think into words. He said that I understand with my heart and Sarah with her head. That I'm different from her, not better or worse."

Gran looked fondly at Worm. "You are a wise little worm, aren't you?"

Worm smiled. "I do my best."

"Which is very good indeed!" Gran laughed. "Use your potions carefully, Boobela."

Boobela thought for a moment. "I never asked . . . how did you make me have a dream about you?"

Gran shook her head and laughed. "That's another story."

A Letter from Mum and Dad

It was the first of the month and Boobela waited impatiently for the postman.

There he was! Even while he was several houses away, Boobela could see the letter sealed with red wax. She opened it eagerly.

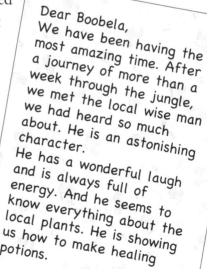

Dear Boobela,

We have been having the most amazing time. After a journey of more than a week through the jungle, we met the local wise man we had heard so much about. He is an astonishing character.

He has a wonderful laugh and is always full of energy. And he seems to know everything about the local plants. He is showing us how to make healing potions.

Boobela thought about how she had just learned to make potions with her gran. Maybe her mum and dad had been making potions at the same time! This made her feel very close to them.

Boobela thought about Gran. She was always full of energy and laughed a lot. She wondered if Gran was a wise woman. She would ask next time she saw her.

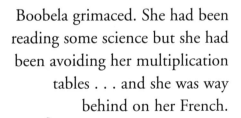

We hope you and Worm are having a good time and that you haven't forgotten your studies. We expect we will have a lot of catching up to do when we get home.

Boobela grimaced. She had been reading some science but she had been avoiding her multiplication tables . . . and she was way behind on her French.

How are Gran and
Granpa? It's very exciting
you have a balloon and
can see them regularly.
We wish you could come
and visit us! But it's far
too dangerous a journey
for a little girl like you.

Boobela smiled. Everyone but her
parents thought of her as an adult
because she was so big. But to her
mum and dad, she was always a
little girl.

Big kisses and lots of
love,

Mum and Dad

P.S. I bet you thought
we'd forgotten about
your Discovery! Of
course not!
Congratulations on
Boobelosa Fantastico!
We're so proud of you!

Boobela sighed and started to read
the letter again from the beginning.

Disappointment Day

Boobela woke with a start. It was eight o'clock already! She'd overslept on this most special of days!

She jumped out of bed and into her best clothes which she'd laid out the night before. Then she ran into the living room. She looked around.

Where was Worm? Where were her presents?

Boobela heard the post drop through the letter box. She ran to the door. Her face fell. Only two letters. Both junk.

No cards. No presents.

Had everybody forgotten it was her birthday? How could they? She'd spent the last two weeks dropping hints.

"It's my birthday next Tuesday. I'll be nine."

A familiar voice interrupted her thoughts.

"There you are, big girl. Happy birthday."

Worm had just crawled into the house through the Worm flap Boobela had put in the back door.

Boobela ran over to him. He didn't *seem* to be carrying anything.

"What should we do today?" asked Worm, like it was a normal day.

Boobela wanted to stamp on the floor and yell: "WHERE ARE MY PRESENTS? WHERE ARE MY CARDS?" But she thought, Worm had *said*, "Happy birthday." Maybe worms don't make a big deal about birthdays.

What about all my other friends? Maybe my birthday isn't such a big deal to them either? she thought sadly.

Boobela felt like a balloon after someone had stuck a pin in. The thing was, it was hard living without her parents and on her birthday she wanted someone to make a fuss of her.

* * *

Boobela decided it would be comforting to be around lots of furry animals. So she and Worm went to a children's zoo.

It was just what she wanted. First, she fed hay to some cows – they nibbled on her fingers, which made her laugh.

At the pig pen, she rubbed the tummy of a big pot-bellied pig called Esmerelda. Esmerelda promptly rolled over and fell asleep.

"You've just hypnotised that pig," said the keeper.

"All I did was tickle her," protested Boobela.

"It doesn't hurt," the keeper laughed. "She likes it!"

And so it seemed. Because a few minutes later, Esmerelda got up and nudged Boobela so she would rub her tummy again.

After hypnotising Esmerelda a couple more times, Boobela went to see the goats.

She wanted to pet the alpaca goat because its fur looked very soft. But its pen had a sign on it saying he sometimes spat. Boobela didn't want to be spat at on her birthday so she gave him a miss.

Then Boobela felt hungry so she and Worm went to the café.

* * *

After lunch, Boobela found a pig-nosed tortoise. He looked very cute. She tried to put it to sleep by tickling his tummy but she couldn't because his tummy was covered with a hard shell.

She found some more goats, with long ears hanging down. These didn't spit so she jumped into their pen. She pretended to butt them and then they chased her around, trying to get her.

Worm looked over her shoulder and warned her whenever a goat was getting near her legs! It was fun!

The goats seemed to enjoy it too.

Then Boobela was tired and decided she wanted to go home.

"What time is it?" asked Worm.

Boobela checked with an adult nearby. "Four o'clock," she replied. "Why do you ask?"

"No reason," said Worm. "You haven't played with the lambs! They're over there." He pointed his head.

Boobela trotted over to the lambs. And this turned out to be the best bit of the day. She was able to hold a tiny lamb in her lap and feed him with a bottle. She loved the way he looked up into her eyes like she was his mum.

After feeding the lamb Worm wanted Boobela to go back to play with the goats.

"I'm tired," she said.

"Please!" said Worm.

"What's up?" Boobela said,
suspiciously.

Worm looked a bit desperate. "I didn't want to tell you," he said. "But a cousin is getting married today and I wasn't invited to the wedding. So I don't want to go home until it's all over."

Boobela gave Worm a sympathetic look. "It's awful not being invited to things! Why didn't you tell me earlier?"

"It's your birthday. I didn't want you to worry," said Worm.

* * *

"Are you sure it's OK to go home now?" Boobela asked. "You don't want to go somewhere else first . . ."

"I'm fine," said Worm. "Stop fussing!"

As they headed up her street, Boobela saw a big van pull away from the front of her house.

She took a sharp breath of air. "Did you see that?"

Worm nodded. "It looked like it was delivering something to your neighbour."

"I thought it was in front of our house," she said.

"Why would a van be in front of our house?" asked Worm.

"It's my b—" Boobela stopped herself. "No reason." She opened the front door and turned on the light.

"Surprise!" shouted Sophie, Jacob, Nurgul, Tom and Kate from the Balloon Club.

"Surprise!" shouted Joey, Rob and the other children from the Volcano Club.

"Happy Birthday," shouted Cheryl and Simon from the beach.

"Oooh la la," shouted Omer, Celine and Sandy from the swimming class.

Boobela was totally amazed. Almost everyone she knew was here. Even the gardener and his wife. Her friends *hadn't* forgotten her birthday!

Boobela looked at Worm who had a twinkle in his eye. "You knew, didn't you? That's why you wanted me to go and play with the goats again! Your cousin wasn't getting married."

Worm laughed. "I had to come up with something."

Boobela couldn't believe her friends had gone to so much trouble.

"Thank you," said Boobela to everyone. And before Worm could get away, she kissed him. "Thank you so much. This must have taken you for ever to plan."

"It was a group effort. But Sophie was the biggest help."

Boobela bent down and gave Sophie a big hug.

She beamed. "You should get changed," she whispered.

Boobela looked at her clothes. She was covered with mud from playing with the goats.

"Worm!" she gasped. "How could you let me get so dirty?"

She ran to her room to find some party clothes.

* * *

By the time she came back, the games had started. There was a string stretched across the room with caramel apples attached.

Nurgul, Joey and Tom were trying to eat the apples without using their hands. Their faces were covered with caramel. They were laughing like wild animals. Boobela joined them. In a moment, her apple was stuck on her forehead!

Near the speakers, Jacob played a song for musical chairs. In the kitchen, Boobela could hear someone making popcorn.

Boobela felt so excited she wanted to do everything at once. She ran towards the popcorn but Sophie blocked her way.

"You're not allowed in here," she said. "Top secret!"

Boobela smiled. She went and bobbed for apples. Her hair got all wet but she didn't care.

Suddenly, the lights went out. Sophie and Nurgul wheeled in a humongous cake from the kitchen. It was actually bigger than them. It had about twenty layers and was covered with strawberry icing, Boobela's favourite.

Everyone started singing "Happy Birthday" and Boobela felt so happy a tear came to her eye. She brushed it away and made a wish. Then she blew out the candles in one big breath.

She looked at all the children surrounding her. "I'm the luckiest giant in the world," she said, "to have so many good friends." She turned to Worm. "And to know such a champion fibber. I never suspected a thing!"

Worm could see the Look in Boobela's eye and he dived into his matchbox.

"No kissing," he shouted.

Sophie gave Boobela the largest knife in the kitchen to cut the first slice of cake. Boobela put it on a plate and held it up. It was absolutely huge.

"Who wants the first one?" she said.

Everyone laughed. No one could eat a piece that big!

"OK," said Boobela. "What if we cut it into three?"

Several children raised their hands. Sophie got a smaller knife and started cutting the cake. As she cut, she talked to Nurgul.

"Ouch," she yelped. She'd cut her finger.

Boobela examined the cut. "Don't worry," she said. "I've made a magic potion that will heal you!"

Boobela ran upstairs and got the golden cream she'd made with Gran.

"It's lovely," said Sophie.

"It's made out of marigolds, sun and beeswax. You'll be the first person to use it."

Boobela got a tissue and wiped the blood off Sophie's finger. Then she applied the potion. Finally, she put on a sticking plaster to keep the cut clean. "It will be better in no time," she said.

"It's almost worth getting my finger cut," said Sophie.

Boobela looked around. The cake was almost half gone and everyone had finished their pieces.

"It's time for the disco," she said to Jacob.

"I was thinking the same thing," he replied.

A moment later music blared out from the huge speakers. The disco ball whirled, reflecting light all around the room. The children started to dance.

After a moment, Boobela wondered where Worm had got to. Her eyes scanned the room. Suddenly, she saw something moving on top of one of the speakers. She looked more closely. It looked like two dancing worms.

Boobela boogied over to the speaker. Worm was wearing his cowboy hat. "I haven't seen that for ages," she said.

"I was saving it for a special occasion, pardner."

Boobela went on, "You haven't introduced me to your friend."

Worm smiled shyly. "This is Hannah. She helped me win the bet about the compost heap."

Boobela made a face. "Grrrr," she growled. "You're responsible for me having to eat vegetables all the time!"

Hannah didn't want a giant to be angry at her. She looked nervous.

"Just joking," Boobela laughed. "I'm pleased to meet you. Any friend of Worm's is a friend of mine!"

* * *

Boobela bopped with Worm and Hannah. Then she moved around the room. She tried to talk to everyone.

Suddenly, Boobela felt very sad. She stopped dancing. Immediately, Sophie came up to her.

"You're thinking about your mum and dad, aren't you?" said Sophie.

"Yes," Boobela replied. "I was wishing they were here." Then she thought a moment. "How did you know?"

"Worm thought this would happen. He said I should keep an eye on you."

Boobela smiled at this. She was so lucky to have such thoughtful friends!

The next day there were loads
of presents to open. And strawberry
birthday cake for breakfast, lunch,
and dinner – for a week!

Look out for …

Boobela and Worm Ride the Waves

Joe Friedman
Illustrated by Sam Childs

Crashing through the waves, twisting
through tunnels and climbing steep cliffs
are some of the challenges ahead for
Boobela and Worm in their latest
collection of adventures, perfect for
reading aloud or together.

Meet the author and illustrator,
and find out more about Boobela
and Worm's world at
www.boobela.com